When you get here

poems by

Akira Olivia Kumamoto

Finishing Line Press
Georgetown, Kentucky

When you get here

Copyright © 2019 by Akira Olivia Kumamoto
ISBN 978-1-63534-922-1 First Edition
All rights reserved under International and Pan-American Copyright Conventions.
No part of this book may be reproduced in any manner whatsoever without written
permission from the publisher, except in the case of brief quotations embodied in
critical articles and reviews.

ACKNOWLEDGMENTS

Thanks and love to Emily Nicol, Iris Miriam Bloomfield, and Joe Wenderoth for their guidance and inspiration throughout this writing process. Thank you to my mom, dad, brother Corin, and the rest of my family, Kumamotos and Cotas alike, for nurturing me into the woman I am today. Thank you to my partner Ben. Thank you to my ancestors/to God. To my all of my friends, old and new, and to those who are no longer in my life but continue to matter to me, thank you. Rest in peace, grandma.

Publisher: Leah Maines
Editor: Christen Kincaid
Cover Art: Akira Olivia Kumamoto
Author Photo: Daniel K. Kim
Cover Design: Leah Huete

Printed in the USA on acid-free paper.
Order online: www.finishinglinepress.com
also available on amazon.com

Author inquiries and mail orders:
Finishing Line Press
P. O. Box 1626
Georgetown, Kentucky 40324
U. S. A.

Table of Contents

A history of fast food 1

Educated Acts of Urban Renewal i-iii 2

Cutting Grandma's Hair 4

Projectile Bleeding 5

Film Theory 6

we are soaked 7

When I am visiting and we are driving through rural
    Maryland at night and you don't notice how dark 8

hard covers [11.9.16] 9

Taking my life 10

Winter Dusk is Pink and Orange and Yellow and Purple
    and Blue 11

A Theory of Everything 12

Cracks in the walls and the cracks in the corners of the
    living room windows 13

Messier 57 14

Re: The Giving Tree 15

soundtrack of the middle of the night 16

It's cold outside 17

I'm a journalist 18

When you get here 20

Prospective Departure 21

A history of fast food

I cried in a Panda Express once.
I think there are ghosts in my apartment.
I spent a month in bed to see if I was alive.
I would never purposely kill myself with a broken shard of In Utero.
I would never purposely kill myself with student loans.
I heard grandpa crying in the dark once and he sounded like the ghosts in my apartment.
I haven't seen my family in a while.
I believe imitation is a compliment but it's really just student loans.
I downed a bottle of Prozac to see if there were ghosts in my apartment.
I doused myself in bleach to see how brown I was.
I tried to untangle the universe once but there were too many student loans.
I am indifferent to the ghosts in Panda Express.

Educated Acts of Urban Renewal i-iii

i.

Little mixed brown girl long tangled brown hair
raccoon hands and raccoon eyes
tips over trashcans trips over trash-lands
scours through precious pearls of wadded foil
hopes she'll find a soda can pop top
'cause her vermin fingers are too thin
for silver or gold or even diamonds in the
rough ruff ruff 'cause she's got the outlook of a bitch
and the in-look of a day-tripper

ii.

I think before jumping and somehow I've never—
but when the brown of dusk settles, it bandages
the slits of the streets
between the high rises and the motels
the liquor stores and the firms
the private boutiques and the smoke shops
the construction and the destruction and the construction and the destruction and the
art and the trash but mostly the art
and I know it'll catch me
off guard and I know that I'll need to be caught off guard
when I rip off that band aid

iii.

She reads poetry 'cause that's what she finds
in the stacks of shit—soliloquies in slimy soup cans,
sonnets under sacks of soda bottles,
like the syntax has been smothered to avoid the
seduction of her starving mind
and when she reads—silver rings slicing her skinny fingers—
she suddenly feels less soulless
like being spoon-fed precious stones,
as blood stains the sentiments ruby red
skin saturated in wounded song

Cutting Grandma's Hair

She thinks we are at Camp Amache and that I am her mother. She tells me the sun is sharp on her skin—that she misses lukewarm San Pedro and the Sunday market on First St.

The strands of her hair are long and thin. They break easily. The silver has long worn to grey, the lackluster of seven unlucky decades at my bronze fingertips.

"母," she says, "cut it short. It is too hot, my head is heavy, I want to run."

It is summer and she is dying. She sits on her balcony in her Dodgers foldout chair, the breeze off the Port of Long Beach drifting through her. She runs her fingers through my hair.

"When we go home one day, I will grow it again, like yours."

She does not want it to get stuck in the barbed wire fence.
I try to cut. I can't.

The sun is sinking below the hills, into the Pacific. She begins to weep, asks me when we can go home. I braid her hair, cut mine, and listen for the Terminal Island foghorn.

Projectile Bleeding

i copied Sylvia once, twice,
and just like her, it didn't work.

i like to pretend I bleed liquid gold
and that if it dries it crusts into diamonds.

reading between the lines only makes you aware that there are too many lines.

they tell you not to rip the knife out of it,
or it'll tear the warm flesh to shreds.

recommended dose is one or two;
we needed more for it to work.

Film Theory

I know that the first minute of a movie about me
would be one long shot
                                          over an array of torn up T-shirts
                            and abandoned mattresses on freeway exits;
the mood:

lacking.

But

there will never be a film—
18 years in front of the 405 North,
                              browning lungs and carbon nail-beds

and nothing can romanticize
mounds of tangled bed sheets,
towers of bloody tissues,
hollow orange plastic pill containers,

cable television and telephone wires fizzling

in the background;

Someone will still yell cut   though
over the traffic's soothing hum
to make sure I am always awake.

we are soaked

and it's raining—
as it's been,

the walls of graffiti
saturated;
bloated letters that
erode to paler hues—
stories gentrified upon storeys
new vowels crumble under—

and it's been raining;

**When I am visiting and we are driving through
rural Maryland at night and you don't notice how dark**

I wonder how many people died over there
in that wooded area just off the road.

The abandoned house, dear,
is just in partial view.
The windows are shattered but still
pick up moonlight.

I wonder if over the decades
they sweat over sawdust
and brick lay
and had a child
with rosy cheeks.

That spot of light, my love,
in the distance:
another home,
perhaps?

Other roads
are not so empty.

I wonder if before the gravel,
they laid here
eyes to the sky
everything agape
glass catching moonlight.

hard covers [11.9.16]

its still
today.

opened my bookcase,
reached out
for Anzaldúa, Angelou, Cha, Silko, Lorde.

unwove the sewn threads
from their aged spines
and stitched the seeping wounds
in my chest, in yours.

the chapters, pages,
they   detached
and settled   gently
on one another.

unbound
i left the window open;
invited in the wind
and moonlight.

Taking my life

Eve, listen
whispers out
fogged window

Winter Dusk Is Pink and Orange and Yellow and Purple and Blue

Sometimes I park behind Davis Sutter Hospital
to cry and watch the sunset.

When it sets completely, there is no light
except for the faint glow of the ER lights.

Sometimes I wander into the barren field
behind the hospital in the dark
and summon the people beneath my feet.

A Theory of Everything

String theory is a theory of everything
and I live in all ten dimensions 'cause I can.

It's like when the tar on the street starts to soften
in 100 degrees and I know that if I walk barefoot across it
I'll come off tougher—
rougher 'cause I feel like it
'cause at this point I can't feel anything in the first dimension
and I only come here when I don't want to feel anything
cooler than 100 degrees.

I think the strings in theory are intertwined in this harmony
that I can't hear 'cause gravity pulls me down in the hierarchy of sonar.

Sometimes he broke things
and when I watched them shatter I saw they never strayed too far from one another
even when glass and shards of wood shot to opposite sides of the room;
'cause as they traveled through all those invisible layers
they got caught in all the same webs, saw all the same spiders,
glossed in the same momentary liminality
that I tried to imagine when I thought about shattering,
and when they landed they returned and taught me
how to stray away so I could see different webs.

Gravity is supposedly a thing I abide by;
I try to loiter in every dimension all at once just 'cause I can.

**Cracks in the walls and the cracks in the corners
of the living room windows**

My main concen is that In
the last amoutn of time

all of us I dom't understand

I don't we cacn't know
of there isnthis Moment

When I am here with you
My friends
I am here don't touch the moment
Me Here we are we can't all of the
Handles us the dark outside as the
streetlights shines Outside in here
We are on thw last straw
And I have thos feeling we are ao la0st
We are infinitebu;llshit we are
Just as we are we

Hanfscoated in cold fireball
We can forget because it's al;

We are blurry and
Aswe speak I know we can ie ypung

Messier 57

I cannot stop ripping
hangnail after nail
hoping the layers never cease.
It's easier when I'm numb
from the brisk evening air
holding me in its selfish caress
diminishing my heat
as I sway
in a child's crouch
in the midst of a dying sun-
flower field off Hwy 113
and stargaze,
neck strained for Cassiopeia,
eyes searching for the invisible
Ring Nebula.
Here is where I can feel
the perished rattling,
freezing in the Earth
beneath me
attempting to seize by soles
and where I must not succumb
to the pressure of hundreds of billions of years
sinking from the sky
resting on my weary shoulders.
Beatles and ants alike ascend on my feet,
climbing to find a peak,
hoping my rough skin is laden with answers
and anecdotes.
Callous winds deafen me—
pain sharp as knowledge
shoots down my spine,
but still I stay
waiting for my sight to adjust
so that I may experience the Ring Nebula
raw
and pray that I do allow the unfeeling all over
to consume me whole.

Re: The Giving Tree

I remember twisting stems
off of leaves,
blood red and yellow,
before they ripped you out
by the roots;
hacked at your trunk,
chipping away at exposed layers
that were trying to age,
to raise limbs,
bare fruit.

I remember picking worms off your corpse,
cradling them in my palms,
burying them in the gaping wound
so they could taste your loamy entrails.

What was left of you petrified
beneath my adolescent nails.
I nestled myself into the cool earth
to see if I could
replace you.

soundtrack of the middle of the night

got new ink today to honor a likely permanence;
no rain tonight, no wind—
nothing through walls
                              grandma talks to the dead in her sleep
                                                400 miles away
                                   slowly suffocating under piles
                     of laundry/junk mail/prospects of infinity
                                                 cannot hear music
picking at the tattoo will make it bleed black
because it is fresh and the itch—the yearn to pick
and pick and pick and pick and
rip off the layers and flake and feel the satisfaction.

                       but there's only quiet

                             grandma talks to the dead in her sleep
                              as if her husband had not succumbed
                                     to Korean war inhalants
                                  and the toxins of the port

grandma talks

to me

in her sleep

it's more melodic
when the soundtrack ends.

It's cold outside

What if I didn't leave the house today
What if I pretend it didn't happen
What if I sliced all my hair off with a pastry cutter
What if I ripped apart the daisy petals with my teeth and catapulted the vase out the window
What if I chipped the paint off the walls with my nails until my fingers bled
What if I ate everything in the fringe including the plastic cartons
What if I said no
What if I emptied the couch cushions and used the fuzz to fill the cracks in the walls
What if I spilled Two Buck Chuck on the kitchen floor for the metaphor
What if I poured Two Buck Chuck on my books for the aesthetic
What if you didn't hear me
What if I overflow the bathtub
What if I flood the toilet
What if I deluge the sink
What if I flush out everything
What if I leave

I'm a journalist

In the morning I use deodorant
to freshen up all the
Bitter
Opinions
I'm not supposed to have.

I wrap my taboos in tin foil,
my tattoos in thread.

My hair used to be a cosmos;
purple, silver, tangled within itself,
always expanding.
It hung in a timeline,
dripping with rancid water
from the tainted pipelines
of the city.

But I've washed away the grit—
the dark matter—
to document what really matters;
blow dried it to hollow straw,
fashioned it to shine brighter
than the flashlights
that found me when I
tripped down the stairs
in the dead of night
because I thought
I heard my
grandmother
crying behind
a barbed-wire fence
in Amache.

--

I stood at the top of the staircase
preparing to jump;
passed the gentle stream of light
that reflected off the wall
nesting shadows of the twisted dark rail
meant to keep me upright
on my way
down.

The first time I'd fallen it was
accidental.
Dark by night;
empty by moon.
I knew I would not die
because I had not prayed for rain.

There was a drought, you see,
and everyone was depending on me:

dad
mom
friend
teacher
you;

and if I did not pray ten times that morning
twelve times that night
rinse my feet in rice vinegar
and sip the blood out of
every wound
on my body

there would be

no rain.

When you get here

I'll brandish my knife for you
if the alleyways and arch of the
St. Vincent Thomas Bridge
casts corpse-like shadows
like the ones that slice between
the rows of red and blue cargo boxes
in clean vertical cuts
and the ones that blanket the filthy freeways—
their somber buzz smothered by
that plague of deserved darkness
and heavy smog.

But I'll need to find a knife,
in the heart of the port
under the pulsating glow of the
blue lights that line the gentle curve of the
St. Vincent Thomas Bridge,
or amongst the ebb and flow of the waves
that glisten gold, reflecting the freeways—
for when I take you to the bridge rails
to show you the navy palette
that spreads past the 110.

Prospective Departure

I squat on the pavement of the platform of the train station at 5 a.m. on Sunday, waiting.

The man at the other end of the terminal is reading a month-old New Yorker under the yellow glow of the streetlights, but his brows are furrowed as if he were drowning in the New York Times' take on the crisis in [insert non-European foreign country here].

My feet are numb, my shoes old, soles thin.

The train-whistle echoes in the distance, the man is fazed and ceases his concern. He stands and joins me on the platform, his body facing North in anticipation.

I have not slept in weeks but I read the news every day. Eyes are heavy. The tracks stretch southward into stillness I can see, past the station into the dark.

The man watches a pinpoint of light emerge into view. He gathers himself and prepares.
I squat low as long as possible, waiting.

Akira Olivia Kumamoto is a poet, essayist, and journalist from Long Beach, California. She studied poetry under the mentorship of Joe Wenderoth at the University of California, Davis, where she graduated summa cum laude with a B.A. in English. Her poems were featured in *The Rumpus* and the *LENNY Letter*'s podcast. She won first prize in the 2015 Pamela Maus Contest in Creative Writing for poetry and was a finalist in the 2015 Ina Coolbrith Poetry Competition.

Akira is Japanese-Mexican/Mestiza American: the descendent of WWII internees, the Tepehuán people of Mexico, Michigan farmers, and Spanish colonizers. She grew up in Long Beach in front of the 405 freeway, and frequently crossed the Vincent Thomas Bridge to San Pedro to visit her grandmother. She's lived in Davis, Berkeley, Manhattan, Brooklyn, and Sacramento and somehow still misses the whir of the early evening traffic behind her childhood home.

She is currently a news video producer for McClatchy, stationed at the *Sacramento Bee*, and holds a Master of Journalism from the University of California, Berkeley. Previously Akira has worked for *NBC News* and *BuzzFeed News*. She is a journalist by day, a poet by night, and 24/7 dog enthusiast. She has a lot of interests.

www.ingramcontent.com/pod-product-compliance
Lightning Source LLC
LaVergne TN
LVHW041525070426
835507LV00013B/1817